FEEDBACK TOOLKIT

Second Edition

16 Tools for Better Communication in the Workplace

FEEDBACK TOOLKIT

Second Edition

16 Tools for Better Communication in the Workplace

Rick Maurer

CRC Press
Taylor & Francis Group
Boca Raton London New York

CRC Press is an imprint of the
Taylor & Francis Group, an **informa** business

A PRODUCTIVITY PRESS BOOK

CRC Press
Taylor & Francis Group
6000 Broken Sound Parkway NW, Suite 300
Boca Raton, FL 33487-2742

ISBN-13: 978-1-4398-4093-1 (pbk)
ISBN-13: 978-1-138-46333-2 (hbk)

Library of Congress Cataloging-in-Publication Data

Maurer, Rick.
    Feedback toolkit : 16 tools for better communication in the workplace / Rick Maurer. -- 2nd ed.
        p. cm.
    Includes bibliographical references and index.
    ISBN 978-1-4398-4093-1 (pbk. : alk. paper)
    1. Communication in personnel management. 2. Feedback (Psychology) I. Title.

HF5549.5.C6M29 2011
658.3'14--dc22
                                                                                2010044389

Visit the Taylor & Francis Web site at
http://www.taylorandfrancis.com

and the CRC Press Web site at
http://www.crcpress.com

Contents

Preface to the Second Edition

As a result of the publication of my first book, *Caught in the Middle* (Productivity Press, 1992), I learned that people were hungry for tools that could assist them in working with others more effectively. Although I listed many tips and suggestions in the book, people seemed to want even more ideas—especially on feedback.

As my consulting practice began to shift its focus to the reasons why people support and resist change, I kept coming back to the importance of person-to-person communication. I found myself coming back to the topic of feedback with fresh eyes. My work with resistance to change, in particular, gave me a deeper and richer way to look at the topic of feedback.

In the first edition of this book, I indicate that dialogue is an important step in the feedback process. I suggest that feedback works best when the giver and receiver realize that they are in a dance together. In other words, I can't give you feedback if I am not willing to consider that I might have a significant hand in creating the performance that we are discussing. Have you ever been on the receiving end of a boss's diatribe about your performance, all the while thinking, "If she got me her comments on time, we wouldn't have this problem"? As I revise *Feedback Toolkit* for this second edition, I feel even more strongly that dialogue is an essential part of the feedback process—and that it is usually absent from these performance conversations.

Some of my friends in the Gestalt community are writing about the negative impact of shame on performance. Most performance conversations in organizations are a breeding ground for shame. Although there are some exceptions, shame shuts most of us down. We perform below our potential. If your organization needs employee and management engagement, then processes that invite shame are working against what you intend to achieve. Dialogue shifts the balance of power from parent to child (or top dog to underdog) to a conversation between two or more people who want the organization to do well.

Here is where the steps of intention and dialogue can meet to support good performance, and build adult-to-adult relationships.

This toolkit is a compilation of ideas that others have shared with me, approaches I developed when I was a coordinator of the feedback process in the Leadership Development Program (a Center for Creative Leadership program) at the University of Maryland, my work at the Gestalt Institute of Cleveland, and tools that I developed or have used successfully with my consulting clients. My thanks to the many people in my life who have demonstrated what it looks like to give and receive feedback well.

Rick Maurer

Acknowledgments

I sent the first draft of the original *Feedback Toolkit* to a number of managers and asked them to use the tools they found useful and valuable. I include some of their comments verbatim in the text. My thanks to Mark Ackelson, Mary Brooks, Douglas DeVries, Margo Freeberg, JoAn Knight Herren, Joe Hill, Richard Hornaday, Gerald Lyner, Sheree Parris Nudd, Leigh Reid, Frank Rodgers, Ruth Voor, and Pat Whelan. (Since I started this project quite a while ago, I imagine I have forgotten others who gave helpful advice. I apologize for any omissions.)

A special thanks to the following for giving me permission to use tools that they either developed or refined: Ellen Harvey for the "'What Are We Doing?' Meeting"; Caela Farren, Beverly Kaye, and Zandy Leibowitz for the "Expectations Exchange"; Mike Korgie for the manager/staff variation; and David Coleman for "Positive Feedback for Teams."

Rick Maurer

About the Author

Rick Maurer is an advisor to leaders in large organizations on ways to plan and implement change successfully. He finds that leaders who can give feedback clearly and directly and receive feedback openly and with interest tend to lead change more effectively.

Many organizations have applied Rick's unique approach to leading change, including the *Washington Post*, Lockheed Martin, Deloitte Consulting, American Management Systems, AARP, Tulane University Hospital and Clinic, Bell Atlantic (Verizon), FAA, Mount Sinai NYU Medical Center, Charles Schwab, Sandia National Labs, Urban Library Institute, National GeoSpatial Intelligence Agency, the District of Columbia Public Schools, the International Monetary Fund, and many other corporations, nonprofits, and federal and local agencies.

His opinion has been sought by the *Wall Street Journal, Fortune*, NBC Nightly News, CNBC, the *Washington Post*, the *New York Times, The Economist, USA Today, Industry Week, Fast Company*, and *Investors' Business Daily*.

In addition to consulting and speaking, Rick teaches at the Gestalt Institute of Cleveland. He is the author of many books on leadership and change, including *Beyond the Wall of Resistance, Why Don't You Want What I Want?* and *The Change without Migraines Formula*. He is also a fledgling part-time jazz musician in the Washington, DC area.

You can contact him at 703-525-7074.

For more information about his work visit www.rickmaurer.com and www.changemanagementnews.com (blog).

1

Using the Toolkit

Always tell the truth, it's the easiest thing to remember.

—**David Mamet**

ABOUT FEEDBACK

In this book, I offer tools to make it easier for people to tell each other the truth as they see it. These tools provide structures—rituals, if you will—that can make it safer for you and your colleagues to engage in honest conversation about critical performance issues.

The tools are like maps—they point the way, warn you about potential trouble spots, and give you a picture of the terrain, but they can't drive the car for you. That's your job. Some trips are easy, scenic, and memorable. Others are like a national lampoon vacation, where everything seems to go wrong.

The better you know the terrain under various driving conditions, the easier it will be for you to anticipate hazards, estimate time, and drive safely.

Feedback is information that lets us know whether you are on or off track. It sounds simple, but, for most of us, it can be quite difficult.

When I first wrote this book, surveys in *Industry Week*[1] indicated that most people in organizations don't get sufficient feedback. The lower you go in an organization, the less feedback is given; the higher you go, the better people think they are doing at giving it. In other words, we believe we do a better job at giving feedback than we really do.

Fast forward to today. It hasn't gotten any better. In fact, it may be worse. Some people supervise people they've never met. It's not uncommon for a single team to span cultures, continents, and time zones. If anything, the pace of work is even faster and more demanding. Conversation seems like a forgotten luxury. Add to that the need for engagement.

Gallup conducts important research on employee engagement. "Research shows that engaged employees are more productive employees." In average companies the ratio of engaged to actively disengaged employees is about 2 to 1. Contrast this to world-class organizations where the ratio of engaged to actively disengaged is 9 to 1.[2] There is a lot that goes into creating a workplace where people are engaged, but employees (and managers) who know what they are supposed to do and have a way to monitor how well they are doing are critical.

Poor feedback leads to performance problems, confusion, wasted effort, anxiety, lower-quality work—and less engagement. I consulted to an organization in which an entire division was confused about how it fit into the company's strategic direction. People didn't know whether they were on target or off, and they found it difficult to get answers to their questions. As a result, when they were in doubt, they simply invented their own performance criteria so that they could feel productive.

Effective feedback can do many things:

Feedback honors competence and reinforces behavior you are looking for.
Feedback helps align expectations and priorities.
Feedback fills gaps in knowledge.
Feedback lets people know where to take corrective action.
Feedback alleviates fear of the unknown.

The handbook is written for you. *Feedback Toolkit* includes many simple tools you can use to improve feedback in your work unit. The tools are informal, and are meant to be adapted to your particular circumstances. Most of them will work just as well whether you are in a paneled corporate office or leaning against a piece of heavy equipment on a shop floor.

Why Feedback Is Tough

A primary focus of my work for the past fifteen years has been resistance to change in organizations. What I have learned applies equally well to the feedback process.

I identified three levels of potential resistance:

Level 1: I don't get what you're talking about.
Level 2: I don't like it.
Level 3: I don't like you.

Obviously, if people don't understand what you're saying, your message isn't going to get across. But that's the easy one to take care of. Levels 2 and 3 are much harder.

Level 2 is an emotional reaction. Something about the feedback process or the feedback I am getting right now strikes fear in me. Adrenalin surges through my body. Negative feedback can mess with our view of ourselves. And that can be frightening. "I'm not as good as I thought I was." "Does this mean I'll lose my job?" "Will I ever be able to do what they want?" And the list goes on.

Level 3 is distrust. I don't believe that the person giving feedback knows enough or is competent enough to give me clear, unbiased feedback.

When level 2 or level 3 gets engaged, the "emotional hijackings," as Daniel Goleman calls it in *Emotional Intelligence*, kicks in and it is difficult for people to take in information.[3] So once the alarms go off and level 2 fear or level 3 distrust rears its head, I can't even hear your logical, detailed level 1 performance review.

What It Takes

Feedback works best when the three levels are working in your favor:

Level 1: I get it.
Level 2: I like it (this seems fair and I can take in what you are saying).
Level 3: I trust you.

I refer to these three levels throughout *Feedback Toolkit*. For more information on the three levels, take a look at my free e-book, *Introduction to Change without Migraines*, available at www.rickmaurer.com.

WHEN FEEDBACK WORKS

Over the years I noticed many things that distinguish managers who have good working relationships with staff from those who are less successful. Not surprisingly, the better managers are generally better at giving and receiving feedback. And most do a good job of paying attention to level 1 information, level 2 emotions, and the level 3 quality of the relationship between them and the people who receive feedback.

Here are a few communication approaches that set the best managers apart:

They just do it. These managers don't wait to become perfect at giving feedback. They know it is important and they just haul off and give it. Sometimes they do it inelegantly, but they earn while they learn and get better with practice.

They give feedback frequently and informally. They don't wait for performance appraisal time—they find many opportunities to give people the information they need.

They focus on the customer. They direct feedback toward making things better for an external customer or for the folks down the hall. This approach keeps the conversation focused on what is truly important and away from personal opinions. These managers know they are in business to serve *customers/clients/users/the public*, and they give feedback with that purpose in mind.

They keep people in the loop. They do a good job of letting people know what's going on. There is great wisdom in the simplicity of open-book management. People need to know the measures that drive the business—from weekly huddles to informal one-page quarterly reports to weekly conversations where people can see where things stand and look at trends. (See "Open-Book Management" in Chapter 2.)

They seek feedback. The best managers find ways to get feedback from their staff. This is a bit surprising, since most organizational structures emphasize top-down feedback and offer no formal way for a boss to receive it. These people have to *work* at getting the feedback they need. They find ways to get around the system. Some organizations create extraordinary mazes through which feedback is supposed to flow. When the formal system doesn't work or creates hassles, these managers take a chance and go around the system. The section on receiving feedback will give you a lot of ways to accomplish this goal.

They build a foundation. These managers realize that the higher the trust level within the office, the easier it is for people to give and receive feedback. They create ways for people to get to know one another, so that feedback sessions aren't meetings between strangers.

WHAT GETS IN THE WAY

As important as it is to realize what works, we must also realize what doesn't work and recognize the ways in which we limit our own effectiveness.

Here are some aspects of management that hinder effective communication of feedback:

Feedback is top-down. In the traditional organizational model, feedback travels only downhill. Even though most performance review systems reinforce this faulty approach, it is critically important to tell the emperor when he or she has forgotten to dress in the morning.

It is not rewarded. You no doubt have heard that what gets rewarded gets done. If giving feedback is viewed as "nice" to do, but not essential, you can't expect people to take the time (and emotional energy) to do it.

Management by exception. We are all busy, and as a result we may give feedback only when something goes wrong. This allows problems to build to a breaking point. And conversely, it makes it too easy to forget to say thank you for the little things. We wait until someone wins a Nobel Prize before we think it's worth our time to say congratulations.

Relying on the performance appraisal system. Performance review is the worst time to give feedback to an employee. You are nervous and the recipient is taking an acid bath. These conditions are not conducive to a productive conversation about performance.

Fear. Fear is a major motivator. We are afraid we might hurt their feelings, or that they might lash out at us. We fear that we don't have all the facts. It doesn't take much fear to give us grand rationalizations for not giving someone feedback at the appropriate time.

We assume they can't think for themselves. Feedback in its purest state simply identifies the behavior and what you'd like to see in the future. But, sometimes we just can't help ourselves and we give people advice on how they should move forward. We give pep talks. Hand them books. Suggest training. Give them the inspirational five-step plan that got us to where we are today. And we give all this free advice without them even having to ask. We feel more like saints than mere managers. We may think we're helping, but what we're actually insulting their intelligence. Unless they ask for advice, don't tell them how to get from A to Z. (This suggestion fits most performance conversations. Obviously, it may not fit conversations with new employees or people who consistently miss the mark.)

I hope that this handbook will help you overcome some of these obstacles—even fear. If you use these tools to give and receive feedback frequently, things won't have a chance to build up. You can begin using feedback as a daily management tool, rather than saving up information to pass on during a dreaded annual performance review. But remember, these tools offer no easy answer. For most of us, giving and receiving feedback is extremely difficult. Respect that. Don't take on more than you or your colleagues can handle.

GENERAL GUIDELINES

Here a few things to keep in mind any time you are preparing to give feedback:

Identify the business reason. Most feedback should be directed toward meeting some business-related goal, for example, to improve the service your unit provides to customers, or to increase efficiency of product delivery.

Ask yourself, "Why is it important to give this person feedback?" If you can't identify a solid business reason, you may be giving feedback for the wrong reasons. You may at times want to give feedback just to clear the air and get something off your chest. That's not feedback; that's venting.

Focus on the future. Too often feedback gets mired in past transgressions. That makes the recipient feel bad and defensive. The past is over. You want performance to improve *in the future*. Give sufficient data about past performance so that the person understands your concern, then discuss how things could be different *in the future*.

Use customer data. When possible, use internal or external customer data as the basis for your feedback. If your organization focuses on meeting customer expectations (and it should), then your feedback helps address this critical challenge. Customer-oriented feedback is far better than feedback that is limited to your opinion of what makes up good or bad performance.

Put it in context. Is this a big issue or a minor problem? A major achievement or a small win? If we launch into the feedback without saying how important it is, the other person's attention is directed on figuring out the severity of the discussion rather than on listening to you.

> Chris, I need to talk with you about project status reports. I want you to know that this isn't a major problem. In fact, I see this discussion as simply fine-tuning.

Early in my career I wrote scripts for training films. I wrote a script to be used to introduce visitors to a robotics demonstration plant. Forty-five minutes into the meeting with my client, we were only on page three of a thirty-page script. He had comments on every line of the script. I thought, "He must hate this script." So, I asked him, "Before we go on, just how bad is this script?" He replied, "It's a fine script, but there's a lot of technical jargon and acronyms that need to be in here to show our visitors that we know the field." I had worked hard to remove jargon thinking they and their visitors would appreciate that. This clarified the overall context—they liked the overall script—and I knew what to do next.

Be specific. Give people tangible examples of the performance you want them to change or continue.

> The status reports are usually three to five days late and are often incomplete with regard to expenditures. Let's look at last week's report. From now on, I would like to get the report on Friday, and I'll need complete budget breakouts in these categories.

Make it timely. If feedback is going to help, it needs to be given near the time of the event. If you wait for months, people may wonder just how important the issue is to you. Timely feedback also ensures that people remember the event. It is hard to discuss something when the other person doesn't recall the details.

Find someplace private. When feedback is negative, people need to be able to save face. Public hangings may feel good to you, but are painful for the people on the receiving end. Even if you believe someone deserves to be criticized in public, your public humiliation of an employee sends a powerful message to the entire staff about you and your leadership style. And that message is: Cover your butt so that you never are the subject of my wrath.

Find someplace public. Although some people are embarrassed by public praise (and you should honor their reticence), usually you should consider criticizing in private, praising in public. Most people like to hear they did well. Public praise can let others know that you appreciate good work.

Consider the risk in giving pubic praise. Some cultures frown on it. You've got to know where you are and who you are working with.

The important thing is that people know that you recognize what they are doing and that you appreciate their work.

Keep it simple and slow. If you have a lot of negative things to say, consider focusing just on the most important concerns. People can take in only so much before they become overwhelmed. If the feedback is detailed, slow down. Give people a chance to take in the information, swallow, and digest it. Even though you may be nervous and want to get the encounter over with, you increase your chances of being heard if you move slowly.

Focus on behavior, not individuals. You are trying to improve or reinforce work performance. Stick with the behavior and avoid personalities. Statements such as "People like you always ..." are needlessly inflammatory.

Explain the impact. Be sure to tell the recipient the impact the behavior is having on you, the organization, and the customer. Let the person know why the issue is important.

> Mary, your delay in getting these chapters to me slows down the entire project. I get behind. My boss keeps asking for my comments on the work, and the editor is forced to work overtime to try to stay close to schedule.

Speak from the heart. The business world is rational. Our meetings are littered with "I think" statements. The language of the head dominates most exchanges at work, and it often serves us well. However, when we have been hurt or betrayed, feel manipulated, or become cautious, this language fails to communicate. We might choose to state our feelings and articulate the pain.

> Pat, when you told me that we could deliver the product on time, I made a promise to the sales team that they could count on having product in the warehouse. You let me down. My word is important to me and now I have to tell them that I was wrong. I don't like to make promises I can't keep.

Speaking from the heart has a strong "it all depends" component. Expressing your feelings can be a powerful way of communicating. It can cut through corporate-speak and get to what is important. In other instances, showing emotion is a sign of weakness. You've got to know the context.

Speak for yourself. Don't act as if you are the spokesperson for the ambiguous *they*. "They aren't too pleased with...." Speak in the first person. Explain how *you* think and feel. Tell the person the impact his or her actions have on you. Be willing to stand behind what you say or don't say it.

Be spontaneous. If you feel an issue should be discussed, you are probably right. Don't wait, do it now. The only exception: If you are angry, wait until your blood pressure drops below 250 to proceed.

Don't inflict feedback. People can take in just so much at one time. Once you exceed what others can handle, they will try to protect themselves from harm. In these situations, you risk never meeting your goals. (See "Don't Forget SARA" in Chapter 3.)

Feedback is much more than just sharing performance information. Feedback can build a relationship between you and your staff in which you can learn to count on each other. Having the courage to tell the truth and ask for it in return increases trust and the ability to work together.

APPLYING THE GUIDELINES

The guidelines described on the preceding pages may seem a bit unwieldy. "I've got to remember to be specific, explain the impact, speak from the heart, be sure to listen, put it in context...."

As a reluctant gunfighter in an old comedy, Bob Hope is forced into a duel at high noon. As he walks down the street, people rush from all sides to offer advice. "He's left-handed, so lean to your right." "He's very tall, so crouch down." "He's very quick, so keep your hand on your gun." As more and more well-wishers give him helpful tips, Hope's walk becomes cluttered with techniques, and his ability to act is increasingly impaired. You may be feeling the same.

Review the guidelines, then don't worry about them—you'll have enough to think about. After the feedback exchange, review the guidelines once again as a way of critiquing what works for you and what can be improved next time.

Here is a simple way to integrate most of the guidelines. I will use this step structure to describe all the tools in this book.

Prepare

Consider the business reason to receive feedback.
Determine the best time and place.
Get the information you need.
Determine how to support yourself.
Consider the context.

Present

Give the business reason for providing feedback.
Offer specific examples.
Explain the impact on the organization and on you personally.

Listen

Hear the other person's point of view.
Listen with open ears.
Be willing to be influenced by what he or she says.

Engage in Dialogue

Hold a conversation.

Listen to each other.

It works best when both parties are deeply interested and curious about the points of view of the other person.

Plan for Action

Search for solutions that you both (or all) can agree to.

Acknowledge

Thank the person and acknowledge what you have accomplished together.

THE IMPORTANCE OF DIALOGUE

Good performance is rarely the result of just a single person doing a phenomenal job. Just ask the support staff for some high-flying salesperson who just got a huge megabonus for landing a big deal. The same is true for bad performance. Have you ever taken a hit for not delivering on something because your boss or colleague didn't hold up his end?

It is easy to forget that good performance is the result of a lot of things working together. W. Edwards Deming knew that. People who study systems know that. Chaos and complexity theorists know that. But performance management systems focus on individuals.

Effective feedback should take context and complexity into account. In other words, if I am giving you feedback about some performance issue, I may have a hand in how well you did.

Most approaches to feedback that I've seen emphasize what you are supposed to say and how you're supposed to say it to the person receiving feedback. Of course that's important, but it's not enough. You need dialogue.

Dialogue should be at the heart of effective feedback. Dialogue is exploration. It is a way of communicating that seeks to make known people's thoughts, feelings, assumptions, and beliefs. It is an exploration into unknown terrain. We learn about others in the process, and are able to test our assumptions about them and their views. In addition, we often begin to learn more about ourselves as we attempt to articulate what we believe. It allows us to see a fuller picture of what's going on.

Tips for Effective Dialogue

The key is being willing to be influenced. Actor and director Alan Alda once said that good actors need to listen with a willingness to be changed. The same is true for leaders.

Here are a few things to consider exploring with the other person when you give feedback:

- What am I doing—or not doing—that is having an impact on your performance? For example:
- Clarity of my directions and feedback?
- Timeliness in getting back to you on key issues?
- My micromanaging or hands-off style?
- Your ability to have access to me?
- The staggering amount of "top-priority assignments" I give you?

What is going on in the organization and the overall environment that might be having an impact on performance? For example:

- How does the overall culture of the organization support or inhibit good performance in this area?
- Access to resources?
- Clarity of overall direction?

It may seem paradoxical, but fully exploring differences often builds relationships. Dialogue builds common ground, as we learn more about who we are in relation to each other. We strip away projections and assumptions and begin to see behind the façades we all erect to protect ourselves.

Dialogue is hard work. It takes discipline. But, it is an effective way to build bridges between people when tensions are high.

Ground Rules You Both Should Follow

1. People must agree to abide by certain rules of conduct in the meeting:
   - Speak for yourself.
   - Maintain confidentiality.
   - Do not make inflammatory comments.
   - Do not attempt to convert others.
   - Show respect for the other person or people.
2. Start easy. Be willing to take it slow and be grateful for even a little candor in the first meeting. Just be aware that open conversation can be risky. Slow is better.
3. Room to explore. Leave sufficient time and space for people to talk. And if you are the type of person who hates dead air and just keeps talking, buy yourself a muzzle.

What to Watch For

Feedback can create a top dog–underdog relationship. One person has all the power and the poor recipient is supposed to sit in gratitude for the pearls that his or her leader offers. This arrogant stance works against good performance. I just learned that a good friend resigned his job working for a member of Congress who was just plain abusive. My buddy is talented and works hard, but he got tired of getting nasty comments in public. He figured he could do better. Organizations lose talented people because they work for leaders who don't get how human beings are supposed to treat other humans. They lose them in other ways as well; performance goes down. There is lots of solid research on the impact of highly engaged employees. Many things contribute to that, but the quality of conversation is a big part of it.

2

Tools for Giving Feedback

Good judgment comes from experience. Experience comes from making bad judgments.

—**Mark Twain**

LEARNING FROM MISTAKES (FOR INDIVIDUALS OR TEAMS)

Mistakes are learning opportunities. Quality improvement gurus such as the late W. Edwards Deming have suggested that over 90% of all performance problems are systems problems. The individual or the team may not be at fault, but something in the overall process makes it difficult to succeed. Perhaps management is giving conflicting messages about priorities, or the computer system breaks down at crucial times, or the system itself is constructed in a way that almost guarantees certain levels of performance.

Consider discussing major breakdowns not as failures, but as *learning opportunities*. If you already have a good process for examining what went wrong, use it. If not, consider the following steps.

Prepare

Before the meeting with the individual or the team, make sure you have a clear picture of what the problem is. These steps are described for a one-on-one meeting but can be adapted for brainstorming with a team. If you can't meet face-to-face, then conduct it over the phone. A web-based call might work well for this so everyone can look at documents together. Although simple, e-mail doesn't lend itself to the spirited back-and-forth interaction you need to make this process work well.

Present

Tell him or her that you want to discuss an important business issue—not to find blame, but to see what both of you can learn from this experience.
  Ask if he or she believes that the issue is worthy of discussion.

Listen

Ask for his or her opinion of what broke down.

- Listen carefully.
- Ask questions that help you understand his or her point of view.
- Don't agree or disagree; just be curious and gather information.

Engage in Dialogue

Give your opinion as to what broke down.
  Talk about the issue. (See "The Importance of Dialogue" in Chapter 1.)

Plan for Action

Identify what both of you can do in the future to minimize the chance that this learning opportunity will turn into a failure.

Acknowledge

Thank him or her for taking part in this discussion.

Variation

When Scott Markey was district claims manager with a large insurance company, he would advertise his own mistakes to his staff. By discussing mistakes as *learning opportunities*, he not only learns ways to improve, but also lets others see that it is better to discuss *failures* than to ignore them.

If you want to apply Scott's idea, use your own learning opportunity as the issue and follow the steps listed above.

What to Watch For

For group brainstorming, it is important to give people time to think about the issues involved before holding a meeting.

We are not used to discussing mistakes with others. Expect people to be reluctant. They may wonder what you are going to do with the information. Will it appear on a performance review? Your first discussion may yield little, but be grateful for what you get, and keep at it.

Once people realize that you are serious and that their honesty will not come back to haunt them, they will participate more openly in these discussions.

Just because you call it a learning opportunity doesn't guarantee that people will see it that way. Being vulnerable at work can be scary. It is the land of level 2 fears and level 3 mistrust: "What will happen to me if I really explain what happened?" (level 2). "Can I trust my boss to not consciously or unconsciously hold this against me sometime in the future?" (level 3).

A "WHAT ARE WE DOING?" MEETING (FOR TEAMS OR WORK GROUPS)

Philip Crosby wrote about *dehassling* the work environment. Here is a very simple technique that might give you a surprising amount of information about the petty hassles that get in the way of high-quality work.

Prepare

No preparation is needed other than making sure you have a room and flip chart or white board to write down responses.

Present

Ask the group to think about the hassles of their daily activities. Then ask the group, "What are *we* doing now that we might be able to *stop* doing?"

This meeting can work just as well virtually, but it may take time for people to warm up. Remember to be patient.

Listen

Everyone—including you—brainstorms ideas. Record the responses on a flip chart or board.

Remember that during the brainstorming, responses are recorded without discussion.

Allow silence. Often people come up with a few ideas and then need time to think. Don't assume silence means that people are finished.

Engage in Dialogue

The entire group sorts the responses. It is likely that each suggestion will fall into one of three categories:

A keeper. Everyone agrees that this activity can be stopped with no negative consequences.

One for consideration. You may question whether an internal or external customer really needs this activity anymore.

Just a dream. It would be wonderful if you could be rid of this activity, but you recognize that you are doomed to repeat it for all eternity.

If there is a disagreement over which category to place a task, the boss should have final say. Unless your organization is completely egalitarian with no hierarchy, then there will be times when the team needs to defer to the leader. If you're the leader, don't say yes to things in this meeting that you know you can't support.

Plan for Action

Clarify (so that everyone understands and agrees) which activities will be eliminated as a result of the meeting.

Determine actions the group will take to explore whether some of the ones for consideration can be eliminated.

Acknowledge

Thank everyone for taking part.

Variation

Consider holding these meetings quarterly. They will help ensure that wasteful activities don't build up.

What to Watch For

Even if the first "What are we doing?" meeting only yields one or two items, it still may be well worth doing. If you handle the meeting well, it can build trust (level 3) and show that you and others are willing to discuss some issues openly (levels 2 and 3).

Don't hold a "What are we doing?" meeting if you feel that suggestion is an implied criticism of you. You'll just make it harder for people to speak candidly about any issues. In other words, you could increase fear and decrease their trust in you.

These meetings can inadvertently threaten people's pet projects. This could evoke level 2 and level 3 reactions against the suggestion.

AN EXPECTATIONS EXCHANGE (FOR INDIVIDUALS OR WORK GROUPS)

This tool is a simple way of getting critical information out on the table. It often takes the threat away from candid conversations. I describe a way groups can engage in this activity under "Variation."

Prepare

Identify the area of work in which you want to give and receive feedback. This could range from all aspects of your work to feedback on a particular project. Make certain there is a sound business reason for the discussion. As much as I prefer face-to-face meetings, an expectations exchange can work very well over the phone.

Present

1. Complete an expectations exchange sheet for the person (or group) you will meet with.

   The other person does the same. Start small. Each person writes just one "more of," "less of," and "keep on doing."
   Here is the expectations exchange format:

   I would like you to do more of _____
       because _____.
   I would like you to do less of _____
       because _____.
   I would like you to keep on doing _____ because
   _____.

2. Someone volunteers to receive feedback first. The other person reads what he or she has written. Read slowly so the recipient is able to take in what you say.

3. Trade places and repeat step 2.

Listen

The feedback recipient asks questions for clarification. While it is OK to answer questions that help clarify what you are reading, it is not OK to justify your requests. What you want the other person to do more or less of is simply what you want. The recipient of your feedback is not obliged to agree with you.

If this process turns into a debate, call a time-out. Remind each other of the "rules" for an expectations exchange.

Engage in Dialogue

Now is the time to discuss points of agreement and disagreement. The first receiver of feedback states what he or she can agree to from the other person's list of expectations. Discuss this. Then the second person describes what he or she can agree to. Discuss that as well.

There should be no expectation that people will agree to everything (or even most of the things) on your list. That's where curiosity and dialogue come in. Get interested in points where you see things similarly and differently. Wonder aloud why you might see things differently. Different priorities? Different pictures of what's expected on a current project?

Plan for Action

Determine what actions each of you will take based on what you learned from the exchange. Determine whether a follow-up meeting is needed.

Acknowledge

Thank the person for taking part in the process.

Variations

Managers with their staff. The manager completes an expectations exchange sheet for the staff as a group. The exchange might begin with, "I would like the staff to take more initiative in...."

The staff meets to create a composite expectations exchange sheet for the manager. Follow the process outlined in the six steps (see p. 10).

In using this variation, remember that people find it very difficult to give candid feedback to a boss. After all, you have control over their performance review, assignments, and pay increases. Read "Guidelines for Receiving Feedback" in Part 3 before using this variation.

Team member–to–team member feedback. I have seen teams use the expectations exchange to make requests of fellow team members. I think it works best if the expectations exchange is limited to one project that is important to the entire team. One team member might make a request to the entire team, "I would like the team to get project updates to me on time because that will allow me to juggle resources and ask for more help if we need it. And, because I won't have to feel like some overcontrolling parent by reminding you things are due." Other expectations may be directed to individuals, "Celia, I'd like you to keep acting as the informal team leader on design issues because we need adult supervision or else things may fall through the cracks."

What to Watch For

Exchange is critical to this process. You must give and receive feedback.

Some managers hold expectations exchange meetings three or four times a year just to make sure the air remains clear.

Be careful. People know how to go through the motions and act like they are being candid and that the process is a valuable use of their time. If level 3 trust is very low, then you need to consider whether this activity will work. You might try a simple variation. The meeting should focus on an issue that is very important to *both of you*. (If the issue is not important to both of you, you are inviting trouble. Why would someone want to be at all vulnerable with someone he or she didn't trust if he or she had nothing to gain from it?) Informally, each of you identifies just one "more of," "less of," and "keep on doing" items.

Trust your gut on this one. If an expectations exchange seems risky to you, maybe you shouldn't do it. For example, this process only works if all parties are willing to be somewhat vulnerable. You have undoubtedly been in work relationships where you didn't trust the other person, and speaking openly and candidly could come back to haunt you.

PROJECT DEBRIEFING (FOR TEAMS)

Project teams need to examine how well they are functioning. Consider this a ten-thousand-mile checkup for your team. This conversation can come at the end of a project or, better yet, at key points throughout the project.

Prepare

Consider the business reason for holding the meeting. Prepare an assessment form and distribute it to everyone on the team. And you may find it helpful to get assessment results from other key stakeholders, such as suppliers and customers.

Here is a list of the types of items you might consider putting on the worksheet.

- To what extent did we meet our goals? Create a 1 to 7 scale: 1 = low and 7 = high.
- What helped? (open-ended question)
- What hindered? (open-ended question)
- What did we learn? (open-ended question)
- What should we change next time? (open-ended question)

If it's a large team (fifteen or more members), collect responses and collate results. Don't interpret or homogenize. It's best for everyone to read what others have to say directly. If you reduce comments like "I was completely out of the loop," "I never knew what was going on," and "I felt like I was a ship in a bad storm without a captain" to a single homogenized bullet point that reads "some communication problems," you will strip the level 2 emotional impact from that important issue.

Present, Listen, and Engage in Dialogue

At the meeting, give people copies of the assessment results. Don't just put the responses on PowerPoint and expect people to remember what's on each slide. Give them copies.

If you gave assessments to other stakeholders, this is the time to present what they had to say.

Go through each item. When you are talking about "what helped," stay on that category until people have had their say, then move on to the next item.

If you have a strong emotional investment in this meeting, ask someone else to facilitate it. You'll be happier and so will the team. And then allow that person to actually facilitate. That means that you will support this person's attempts to move the discussion on to the next point or to make sure all voices are heard or to put a cork in your mouth when you start to dominate the conversation.

Through dialogue, get beneath the surface. As Chris Argyrus suggests, "discuss the undiscussable issues."[4] Some might call this the elephant in the room. The facilitator needs to create conditions so that people can explore these unspeakable truths about the work you do. Be sure to review the section on engaging in dialogue before the meeting.

Plan for Action

If this is a ten-thousand-mile checkup, then the task is simple:

- What did we learn from this assessment process?
- What will we keep on doing and do differently as a result?

If this is an end-of-the-project review, then the task is:

- What did we learn?
- What do we need to remember on the next project?

Acknowledge

Thank people for taking part in this.

What to Watch For

When level 2 fears and level 3 distrust are high, it will be difficult to get good information from this assessment process. Sometimes you may not know that fears are that strong until you engage in a meeting like this that just falls flat. One way to tell that it's not working: there is no emotion in the room. (Emotions can be excitement and engagement as well as expressions of fear or anger.) Everything is polite level 1 information. If you find yourself getting bored, that may be a signal that this meeting is not working. If that happens, thank people for their involvement and then find ways to learn what you need to know about the project in other ways, such as anonymous surveys, one-on-one informal chats, and management by wandering around (see description of that tool below).

Addressing level 2 fears and level 3 lack of trust is beyond the scope of this short toolkit. You might be interested in a book I wrote that explores the three levels deeply: *Why Don't You Want What I Want?*[5]

Variations

After action reports (AARs) were developed by the military. (Some would say that Julius Caesar's *Commentaries on the Gallic War* was the first after action report.) An AAR is a rigorous process to determine what worked and what didn't. It explores (1) what needs improvement, (2) establishing plans and tangible measurements to address deficiencies, and (3) what did we learn?

If you do a Google search on the phrase "after action report," you will find sample AARs and guidelines for engaging in this process. I urge you to look at these samples and then design your own process and goals so that the AAR addresses issues that are important to you and your customers.

HOW'S OUR TEAM DOING? (FOR TEAMS)

Prepare

Sometimes it can be helpful for a team to examine how well it is working together on the basic things that are expected of teams. This process can be especially important for virtual teams. When you are on a virtual team, it is easy to let seemingly minor problems build.

Here are some items that might get you thinking. You may find things to add or delete.

- Clarity of our mission
- How well we meet our goals
- Clarity of our respective roles
- How well we communicate
  - Keep each other informed
  - Provide feedback to each other
  - Share lessons learned and things to watch out for
- Efficiency and effectiveness of our meetings
- Effectiveness of our decision-making process
- How well we handle conflict on the team
- How we acknowledge our individual and collective accomplishments
- Extent to which the way we are organized supports effective work
- Extent to which we are viewed favorably (level 3) by our key stakeholders

Present and Listen

Ask everyone to rate each item on a scale of 1 to 5 (1 = poor, 5 = great). And you should rate the team as well.

Ask each individual to state the grade he or she gave the group. Don't discuss the reasons for scores until everyone has given his or her score.

Ask each team member to explain the reasons for the grade he or she gave. Don't discuss or debate scores; simply listen.

Make sure people listen to each other. Resist the temptation to influence their opinions.

Engage in Dialogue

Discuss:

> What is working well on the team?
> What is hindering our effectiveness?

Plan for Action

Identify actions the team can take to improve or maintain good performance in the future.

Acknowledge

Ask people what they thought of the process. Thank them for taking part.

What to Watch For

Often when teams discuss work, they focus exclusively on the project and fail to address how they are working together. This exercise asks you to examine both aspects. How a team works together has a major impact on the quality of the work it does. The team may resist talking about itself, but it is worth pushing. During the first ten-thousand-mile checkup, conversation about the team may be superficial. That's fine. People are cautious. Next time they may say more.

This tool should not be an excuse to dump on people. Stick to the business reasons for this "How are we doing?" meeting.

If one person's scores are significantly different from those of other members on the team, the group may exert subtle pressure to get the wayward soul back in line. Resist the temptation to convert, since minority viewpoints provide valuable information. The way in which this person sees the world is true for him or her.

The leader should speak last. As one manager said, "Watch out for subtle domination by the team leader." People are likely to defer to you.

One manager told me, "I found better-quality feedback when the team leader's or facilitator's remarks were given last. I tried both ways, and feel that my comments influenced the group when I gave them early."

Be careful not to overreact. If people start blaming you for all the ills of the world, you may get defensive and say something you will later regret. Just listen and ask for clarification. This too shall pass.

Encourage everyone to speak. Facilitate the discussion to make sure it is truly a team debriefing and not just an opportunity for soapbox oratory from one person.

MANAGEMENT BY WANDERING AROUND (FOR INDIVIDUALS)

Peters and Waterman described *management by wandering around* (MBWA) in their seminal book, *In Search of Excellence*.[3] Unfortunately, something sad happens in organizations. Once an idea like MBWA, paradigm shift, empowerment, or total quality management (TQM) gets some age to it, we believe it's lost its value. We tire of the term well before we understand the concept. If your organization suffers from this fascination with the latest buzzword, get over it. Forget that MBWA is old; it still works. It is informal, allows you to give and receive information, and makes you accessible to your staff.

Prepare

Don't prepare. You shouldn't wander with a purpose. There is a difference between wandering around and making a beeline. If each time you make your informal stroll you zing someone, it won't be long before people become wary of your presence.

Present, Listen, and Engage in Dialogue

Follow your interests and curiosity. Talk, listen, and engage as the spirit moves you. The less you plan, the more effective MBWA will be.

Keep your eyes open. What's working? What isn't?

Acknowledge good work.

Make suggestions for fine-tuning if you can do so privately. If not, save the feedback for later.

Be curious. Ask questions.

Get to know your staff.

Plan for Action

As a result of the wandering, make notes about things you need to take action on. Perhaps you made a promise to someone or saw a quality problem needing attention.

Get back to people. If you say you'll follow up on something, keep your word.

Acknowledge

Except for a simple thank you to people as you walk around, no other acknowledgment is necessary.

Variations

If your staff is housed in various locations on other continents, you may need to be creative. One manager uses e-mail frequently and informally to stay in touch with his staff. But, as you know, e-mail can be overused. If you e-mail for MBWA, consider just asking one question to the person you are writing to. And don't send to a group; send a personal note to a single person. "Hey, I was wondering how the new machine was working out for you? Any feedback for me, or is there anything I can do to help?"

Or pick up a phone and ask that same question.

Neither of these variations work as well as face-to-face, but many of you don't have that luxury these days.

What to Watch For

Be careful not to jump over the chain of command and create other staff problems by interfering in people's work.

The first time you wander, people may not speak candidly. They may think, "Oh, he just read another management book." Be patient and keep wandering.

One manager suggests that MBWA needs to become a habit. If you only walk around occasionally, it is inevitably a big deal and your associates will be uncomfortable. By making MBWA a part of your weekly schedule, your associates will relax, you will see what is really happening, and your feedback will be used on the *real* process, not just the process that's followed when the boss is around.

I once suggested this tool to a client who was woefully out of touch with her staff. She replied, "I tried it once and it didn't work." Wandering only once won't do much good. People must get used to seeing you around.

POSITIVE FEEDBACK FOR TEAMS (TEAMS OR WORK GROUPS)

Most people receive precious little emotional support at work. Except for the occasional thank you and rubber chicken dinner, the workplace is often barren of significant positive feedback. This saps the spirit of most. People need to feel appreciated.

The following exercise is wonderful. I have seen people deeply moved by it. People may be reluctant, however, to take part in something that seems so touchy-feely. If you work on a team that could use a dose of positive reinforcement, you might consider it. Sadly, some workplaces are so devoid of emotion that this exercise would be derided. Too bad for them.

Prepare

No preparation is needed, other than to make sure people are willing to take part.

Present

Ask each member of the group to write his or her name on top of a blank sheet of paper and pass it to the left.

Each person writes one sentence about this person that begins, "I appreciate ...," "I admire ...," or "I respect...." For example, one person may write, "I appreciate your willingness to stay until the job gets done."

The sheets are passed to the left once again, and each team member writes a sentence on the new sheet.

Continue this process until everyone has his or her own sheet back again. Each person should scan the comments received.

One person volunteers to pass his or her sheet around for oral comments. As it makes the rounds, each person reads the sentence he or she wrote and expands on it. For instance, someone might say, "I wrote, 'I appreciate your willingness to stay until the job is done.' Often during the past few months you have stayed here well beyond closing time to make sure everything was ready to go out the next morning. That saved me a lot of headaches. Thanks."

Repeat the process so that everyone's written comments are read aloud.

Listen

During this process, the recipient of the feedback has a very simple job— shut up and listen. So often we talk away positive feedback—making excuses, giving credit to others, or telling the feedback givers why they are wrong. Don't allow that to happen, it just saps the energy from this process.

Engage in Dialogue

No dialogue is needed.

Plan for Action

No action is needed.

Acknowledge

Hold a brief discussion. Ask people, "What did you think of this exercise?"

Variation

Post blank flip chart sheets around the room. Each person's name is written on a sheet. Individuals write comments randomly, using different colored markers. At the end of the exercise, the individual accepts and reads his or her sheet. This approach works well for a large team.

What to Watch For

Don't force this tool on an unsuspecting group. Make sure people are willing to engage in it before you begin. That doesn't mean you shouldn't nudge them—simply don't inflict it on them.

Monitor the process. Make certain that recipients remain silent except to ask questions for clarification. The only declarative sentence allowed is "Thank you."

CONDUCTING A PERFORMANCE REVIEW

> Evaluation of performance, merit rating, or annual review ... The idea of a merit rating is alluring. The sound of the words captivates the imagination: pay for what you get; get what you pay for; motivate people to do their best, for their own good. The effect is exactly the opposite of what the words promise.
>
> **—W. Edwards Deming,** *Out of the Crisis* (p. 101)

I hate performance appraisals. They work against the very thing we desire— improved performance. Peter Block, W. Edwards Deming, Philip Crosby, and Stephen Covey have harangued against them, and if they couldn't change organizations' fascination with this annual bloodletting ritual, I don't imagine my words will help much either. Nevertheless, I'll try.

Most performance review systems reinforce a paternalistic world, one built on distrust and the assumption that the boss knows more about our skills, abilities, and commitment than we do. This dependency works against empowerment and engagement. And focusing on individual performance problems, rather than looking at systems issues, works against the grain of quality improvement.

If you agree with this view and can influence your organization to change, go for it. Or if you can get around the system and avoid performance reviews, I wish you well. However, if you are a manager caught in the middle somewhere, with little power to change the system, at least consider the following ideas. They might help make your performance reviews a little more humane and maybe even helpful.

Prepare

First, consider levels 1, 2, and 3 as you prepare. Most performance management systems act as if they are strictly rational and objective level 1 affairs. They are anything but level 1. Think about when you are on the receiving end: Adrenalin surges through your body, getting you ready for the worst. Should you flee, fight, or stand really still (like a deer in headlights) so that the reviewer won't see you? Appreciate the fact that all three levels will be alive in the person you are about to meet with.

And these levels will be alive for you as the bearer of this news. You may try to hide behind the objective-looking level 1 feedback form, but inside you are roiling. You may be thinking, "I hope I make it through this one alive or at least intact."

Heightened emotions can lead us to say and do things that we regret later. We may get too forceful and make our points a little too strongly (fight), or give in and give them a sugar-coated report (flight), or talk around the issues, complaining about how bad the system is or asking about the kids, sports, weather, or their move from Chicago (flight and deer in the headlights). That's why preparation is so essential.

At level 3 you need to ask yourself, do you have standing to offer feedback that this other person will take seriously? If not, then think about how to make this meeting one in which to begin building the bridge between you just a little bit. And don't set too high of expectations on yourself. When the negative side of level 3 is engaged, the person isn't listening to you anyhow.

Do your homework. As Yogi Berra once said, "You've got to have deep depth." Do whatever it takes to find specific examples illustrating the points you want to make.

Support yourself. Consider how you will feel during the session. Determine ways to support yourself. Take time to review your notes prior to the meeting. Rehearse. Do something (short of guzzling cheap booze) so that you feel as relaxed and centered as possible going into the review. For example, you might take a short walk, sit quietly for a few moments, or take a few deep breaths. And during the meeting, remember to breathe.

Consider how you will support the recipient of the performance review. These reviews can be stressful for everyone. Put yourself in this person's shoes for a moment. How would you feel if you were about to receive this feedback? Is there anything you can do to make it easier for him or her to take in the information and engage in a meaningful conversation with you about performance?

Present

Stick to the point. Cato the Censor said, "Stick to the point and the words will take care of themselves." Prior to the meeting, decide what points you need to make. Be aware of what nervousness does to your own best intentions.

Keep it simple and clear. There should be no surprises during a performance review. (If there are, apologize and promise to do better in the future.) Make your point. Give an example or two. Use customer information. Use data from your customers and other stakeholders as the basis for the review. These people are the reason you exist. Their comments should guide feedback. Also consider discussing those adaptive skills that have an impact on the work. (See "Preparing to Receive Feedback" in Chapter 3 for a description of these skills.)

Listen

Shut up. Stop talking and make certain the recipient understands what you have said. You might ask him or her to paraphrase your comments.

Pace yourself. People can take in only so much before they are overwhelmed. Go slowly. Allow the recipient to respond, breathe, and ask questions. Out of nervousness, you may be inclined to rush the meeting simply to get the onerous event over with until next year.

Engage in Dialogue

Build a partnership. Ask, "How can I assist you?" Find ways to help staff be successful. I don't mean that you do their job, but you might be a liaison to other units, coordinate workflow within the department, or work with suppliers to make sure resources get to your staff on time. This is an opportunity for you to receive feedback too.

Avoid grades. No one wants to get a B or a C. People translate number scales into letter grades. A students who fail to receive As as a result of an arbitrary quota system will be hurt and furious. B and C students who receive these grades, even though accurate, will begin to live down to your expectations. I realize that many systems require you to give grades. Some sick review systems even set quotas for the number of top grades you are allowed to give (so much for empowerment). I encourage you to do what you can to get around the system and still keep your job.

Discuss the system. Since most performance problems are the result of a system flaw rather than a person's commitment, abilities, or skills, attention that is so focused on the individual seems misplaced. Discuss what needs to be changed to support this person in doing excellent work.

Plan for Action

Focus on the future. The purpose of most performance appraisals is to improve performance in the future. Get off past events as quickly as possible, and discuss ways you can work together better in the future.

Acknowledge

Thank the other person for engaging in the discussion.

What to Watch For

Don't ignore the potential power of level 2 emotions and the level 3 relationship with the other person. These things matter deeply. Two big mistakes you can make: (1) assume that performance discussions are rational level 1, and if you can provide enough data, all is well, and (2) there should be no surprises in a formal review. If people are surprised by your assessment of their work, you haven't been doing your job the other 364 days.

ACID BATH FEEDBACK

At times giving feedback can be difficult, painful, and necessary.

Prepare

Make certain you can give a specific example or two to back up whatever point you want to make.

Identify any way in which you might be contributing to the problem.

Rehearse. Imagine what typically happens when you talk with this person about something that might cause stomach acid to flow. Or imagine your worst fear. I say X, he loses his temper, and then I do something stupid. Then things get really bad. If that's the only picture you've got of what might happen as you walk into that meeting, you're not likely to come up with some grand way of engaging this person on the spot. You've got to practice. Think about options and rehearse using them. You can practice privately and silently. Rehearsing doing things "the right way" begins to anchor those options, so in the heat of the moment you are more likely to be able to draw on that wisdom.

Get coaching. You don't need to go to a professional coach (although they can be very good). Just talking it through with someone you trust often can help.

Do whatever it takes to support yourself during the meeting—ninjas standing guard outside your door, whatever.

Present

Stick to the point. Keep your goal in mind. Don't be distracted by seductive side conversations. Going off on a tangent is simply a way for both of you to avoid the major issues.

Keep the feedback simple and clear. Go into the meeting prepared to talk about one or two points. Don't include everything you have ever wanted to say to this person.

Use real data. Use customer and other stakeholder data as the basis for feedback. Avoid giving opinions or speculating.

Breathe deeply and often. People often hold their breath in tense moments. That's a real bad idea. The good news is that just noticing your breath may help you get a bit calmer.

Listen

Go slowly. Think of an old steam boiler with its pressure release valve. When things begin to heat up, you both need to be able to cool down. Allow silence. Time to breathe. Time for the other person to respond. You can consider taking a break, but acid bath feedback meetings seem to work best when they are short. (Just how much can you and the other person take before it isn't much fun anymore?)

Engage in Dialogue

In some instances, the feedback needs to go both ways. In those cases, use this as an opportunity to build a partnership. Discuss your own role in improving performance in the future. Take responsibility for your part of the problem. If you don't see yourself as part of the problem, think again before inflicting your thoughts on the other person. Problems are seldom one-sided.

If this feedback meeting is one of many such meetings with this person, and he or she still doesn't get it, then you may not want to engage in dialogue. In those rare instances, give the feedback, make sure you were understood, talk about consequences (if appropriate), and then end the meeting.

Plan for Action

The past is gone, and you want things to improve in the future. Remember, it is hard to be defensive about the future since it hasn't happened yet.

What to Watch For

Acid bath feedback lives in the land of fierce level 2 and level 3 emotions and reactions. Just thinking about one of these meetings can cause us to react physically. That's why thinking about the meeting and practicing can help. If you meditate or do relaxation exercises or find physical exercise calming, do it now. The more calm and present you can be during the acid bath meeting, the more options you will have.

And decide if you want this to be a two-way conversation so that you receive feedback as well. If not, then structure the meeting so that doesn't happen.

PROVIDING FEEDBACK AS A MENTOR

The role of a mentor can be critically important to the career of those mentored. The role of the mentor is to help the mentees see how things get done in the organization, how they can get things done, and pitfalls to avoid. Feedback and advice play a big role in this relationship.

Preparation

You need to know enough about the person you are mentoring to be able to provide good feedback. Therefore, you need to see him or her in action. You need to see this person in staff meetings, working a project, and get a sense of how others are responding to him or her. Preparation is an ongoing process.

Present, Listen, and Engage in Dialogue

I think meetings between mentors and mentees should have some structure but space for free-ranging conversations. Only part of that involves feedback.

Generally, I think the mentee should say what he or she is looking for with regard to feedback. It is that person's career, so it is important that he or she keeps his or her eyes open regarding what's important.

And, it is the mentor's responsibility (that would be you) to impose what you notice on the mentee. If it seems that the mentee is failing to seek out opportunities or only half showing up for meetings, it is your job to say that. More than anywhere else, you should feel free to play your hunches. If you have an inkling that the mentee needs to focus on something, say it.

This is where dialogue comes in. Both of you can then explore this issue more deeply. The give and take of conversation is key.

Identify, Analyze, and Generalize (IAG)

I learned this many years ago when I was first getting training at MATC (a long defunct organization, sad to say) in working with groups and organizations. It provides a good way for you and your mentee to talk about critical incidents in his or her professional life.

Identify. The mentee identifies a specific moment that she wants to debrief. If she says she wants to talk about the four-hour presentation she made to regional staff last week, ask her to pick out a specific moment that stands out. Trying to debrief all the work that went into planning and then the event itself is too much. Asking her to identify a moment that seems to be important often can be the seed for a rich discussion. And later, if you want to explore the entire event, go for it.

Analyze. Help your mentee examine what went on dispassionately. Encourage her to leave judgments out. "No, I messed up" statements are allowed.

- What did you say or do?
- What did others says or do?
- What was the impact?
- And so on.

Generalize. Ask the mentee what he learned. You can add anything you just learned as well. And then ask, "So where else might what you learned apply?"

Plan for Action

Encourage your mentee to apply what he or she is learning. Set up experiments so he or she can test his or her skills.

What to Watch For

The relationship between mentor and mentee should have juice in it—it should feel dynamic. If it doesn't, talk about it. Just because the gods of management forced you together doesn't mean that you are a good pair for each other.

One very good test: Are you finding working with this person fun or engaging? If not, it's time for a conversation. Your indifference, boredom, whatever, could be the germ of something important that your mentee needs to hear.

OPEN-BOOK MANAGEMENT (TEAM)

Open-book management is a great way to give teams feedback. The concept is simple: organizations that use open-book management simply open the books so people can see the numbers that drive the business.

This can be used as a tool for running the team or organization, or can be used for specific processes like Lean, Six Sigma, and other improvement processes.

Prepare

Learn something about open-book management before you begin. There are rough guidelines that will allow you to customize an approach that works for you. Consider reading *The Open Book Experience*[7] by John Case for lots of examples of how it can work. Or, read Jack Stack's *The Great Game of Business*,[8] which got a lot of people interested in the potential of opening the books.

Then you will need to create a way to open the books that makes sense to you and your organization. Ask yourself:

- What are the critical numbers that people need to know?
- What's a good way to get this information to people in a timely manner?
- What's my plan for ensuring that people make the connection between the numbers and their own work?
- How will we keep ourselves accountable?

Present

The Great Game of Business (a firm started by Jack Stack) developed a simple and elegant approach. Groups get together once or twice a week in a huddle. It's called a huddle because it is quick and no one sits down. It is not a typical meeting where people look at their watches hoping to escape.

Each person is responsible for meeting some number. Each member of the team says this was my number for the week, here's how I did, and here's why. On to the next person. No retributions. No long conversations. But knowing that each week at a specified time the team will huddle and go over numbers gets people's attention.

You might do a Google search on "weekly huddle" to see how organizations like the Container Store use it.

Listen and Engage in Dialogue

Whatever process you use, attention to listening is critical. Open books suggest that the process is open. Everyone sees everything that is relevant to making the business successful.

Plan for Action

This may or may not apply given the way you structure things.

Acknowledge

Always thank people.

Variations

There are countless variations. I encourage you to read any of the fine books by John Case to see the wide variety of ways people apply the principles of opening the books. You'll find that there is no one-size-fits-all approach. Many organizations invent their own approach. I love the grassroots nature of the open-book approach.

What to Watch For

If you provide data that your team can't understand, you might as well keep the books closed. It is important to make information available in ways that people understand it (level 1). Some organizations provide training on how to read a balance sheet and so forth.

It takes trust in your staff to open the books. You may fear that they will misuse the information or will be overwhelmed. In my experience, people who open the books love it. But, don't do it if you think you might pull the plug. Once you allow transparency, it's almost impossible to close the books. You can probably see that although the critical number (level 1) is important, level 2 excitement or fear and level 3 trust or distrust can make or break the process.

3

Tools for Receiving Feedback

To influence, we must be willing to be influenced.

—Anonymous

PREPARING TO RECEIVE FEEDBACK

Throughout this toolkit, I have urged you to ask for feedback that is job related. Although using these tools will get at important issues, you may not hear important feedback about your own work. If, for instance, your approach to working with staff rivals Genghis Khan's, people will be reluctant to speak candidly. And the feedback you do receive will never address the underlying problem. Consequently, you will get a false sense of what is real.

The Leadership Institute of Seattle (LIOS) and Richard Bolles developed a model that speaks to this dilemma.[9] The skills we need at work are divided into three major categories:

Work content skills. These are the specific skills needed to perform a particular job. For an engineer, they are all the specific skills that go with engineering. When good feedback is given at work, it usually relates to work content skills, since others are most comfortable talking about an area where measurement is so clear.

Functional skills. These skills, which are more transferable from job to job, include the ability to run a meeting, lead a project team, make a briefing, give speeches, and so forth. Often we receive little feedback in this area. This handbook may help you address many of the functional skills you need.

Adaptive skills. These are basic, getting along with people skills. As former LIOS associate John Runyon once said, "They are things we hope our children learn, but no one ever teaches."

Adaptive skills can help you perform the other skill sets effectively. Neglect or misuse of these skills can seriously impede your performance—and can even threaten your career.

Here are some adaptive skills that I believe are important for managers. A study at the Center for Creative Leadership found that poor adaptive skills were a significant reason why the careers of executives derailed.

Be straightforward. During the height of the Reagan era, Barry Goldwater, the patriarch of American conservatives in this country, said he believed that the best president of the past one hundred years was the liberal Democrat Harry S. Truman. He said, "I never went to bed at night wondering where Harry stood on anything." With straightforward people, *what you see is what you get.*[10]

Keep things in perspective. People with a big-picture viewpoint are able to take their work seriously, while not taking themselves too seriously. They are the calm within the storm. We all know people whose sole contribution to a raging fire is to bring gasoline, while others seem to handle every crisis confidently and calmly.

In the 1983 World Series, Philadelphia Phillies short-reliever Tug McGraw pitched brilliantly in late-inning situations. But as he left the field his pitching arm would tremble wildly. Reporters asked how he could pitch so well when he seemed so nervous. He said that when he began to get tense on the mound, he would say to himself, "Someday, when our sun goes supernova and the world turns to a ball of ice, what difference will this pitch have made?" Then he pitched the ball.

Keep commitments. With these people, their word is their bond. If they say they will have a draft to you by Friday at 4:00, you know it will be on your desk on time.

Be aware of impact on others. Some people, while far from perfect, know the impact they have on others. This quality allows them to hold their weaknesses in check and take corrective action when they blow it. Joe Bltsplk, a pathetic creature in Al Capp's "Lil Abner" comic strip, personified the antithesis of this skill. Wherever he appeared, trains collided, businesses went belly-up, and robberies increased. Joe meandered through life, oblivious to the fact that his presence caused these disasters. Organizations are filled with Joe's cousins. To avoid being one, take a look at your responses as if you were in the other person's shoes.

Be sensitive to people. Some managers work as if they believe in the golden rule, treating others with dignity and respect. Although other "textbook managers" seem to do all the right things, their style and manner with others is abrasive. Their praise is hollow. Their disdain for others is apparent. Be sincere—you and your colleagues will know the difference.

Be able to self-correct. In my study of effective middle management practices, I found that the best managers were not perfect human beings by any means, but they did have a capacity and desire to learn from their mistakes.

This list of adaptive skills is not definitive. I encourage you to create your own list. Look around you. What are the things people say behind others' backs? As you look at poor Bernie drooling in the corner, consider the reasons why his career stalled years ago. Why do people like working with Sally, and why does she excel where others fail? This informal assessment will help you begin to see which adaptive skills are critical for success in your organization.

Asking for feedback on your own adaptive skills is difficult. Most aren't comfortable talking about such *personal* issues, yet these skills are essential. Since others are likely to avoid telling you what everyone already knows, getting feedback can be tricky. The guidelines listed on the following pages are particularly important with regard to these skills.

GUIDELINES FOR RECEIVING FEEDBACK

Determine if you want to hear feedback on work content, functional, or adaptive skills. Use the following guidelines in combination with the other tools in this section to make sure you receive the best possible feedback from these encounters.

Place clear boundaries around the feedback. Let people know what you want and how much feedback you are prepared to hear today. If you fail to define precisely what you want and who you want to hear from, you run the risk of hearing too much unfocused information. Once that happens, you may get defensive. You may shut down and close the others out, or you may lash out at those who are trying to tell the truth as they see it. In either case, it will be far more difficult for people to be candid in the future.

Listen beneath the words. Listen for subtle cues embedded in the feedback you receive on work content and functional skills. You may hear a phrase—or something in a person's voice—that indicates a potential adaptive skill problem. People feel most comfortable giving you level 1 feedback: just the data. What you need to listen for is their probable emotional reaction to what they are telling you (level 2).

Explore gently. You might ask, "Is there anything in my style that is getting in the way of our meeting this goal?" You may receive no feedback or you may hear a polite comment that begins to touch on an adaptive skill. Be grateful and consider what the person said. Since this gets into level 3 territory, it may be hard for people to say things that are critical. Don't push people to give you feedback if it seems that they may feel it's a risky endeavor for them.

Don't defend yourself. If you want feedback, you must accept that what others tell you is true from their vantage point. You don't have to believe it. You aren't obligated to do anything differently as a result of hearing it, but you must listen openly. At the first sign that you are defending your actions, others will likely stop telling you their truth.

Express your thanks. Let people know you appreciate their candor. After you have had time to think about the feedback, tell them ways in which the feedback was helpful.

DON'T FORGET SARA

Feedback can be overwhelming. When this happens, you are likely to experience its impact in stages. Understanding this natural progression of reactions may help you deal with the news more calmly—and keep you from taking some action you may regret. So, when you receive feedback, think of SARA. It stands for surprise, anger, rationalization, and acceptance.

Surprise

When you first hear feedback, you may be surprised or shocked. You may not be sure how to respond. This reaction is natural and healthy. You are simply protecting yourself from taking in too much too quickly. Honor this response.

When you are surprised, the best action is no action. Allow yourself time to experience surprise. Don't try to make decisions or plans—simply trust that this feeling will pass.

Anger

Surprise is often replaced by anger. "How can they say that to me!" If the feedback came anonymously, you may wonder, "Who said what?" Once again, anger is natural and will pass. Enjoy the ride.

Don't take any action while you are feeling angry. You will only do damage.

Rationalization

During rationalization, you are likely to make excuses for your actions and come up with very *thoughtful* reasons why the person who gave you feedback was a dolt who couldn't see excellence if it bit him. Your statements sound rational, almost as if you are back in control. You may sound logical and all together, but you aren't.

During this phase you may try to make sense of the feedback by making excuses. "Well, I wasn't surprised they rated me low on planning. After all, they've only known me for seven years. Once they get to know my work…." Once again, just recognize that you are probably rationalizing and don't do anything.

Acceptance

You can now look at the feedback with some degree of objectivity, take what is useful, and disregard the rest. You can digest what you've heard and determine what provides nourishment and what should be eliminated.

We cannot rush SARA, she moves at her own pace. When feedback is overwhelming or particularly surprising, we may find ourselves remaining in surprise and anger for a long time. At other times, we may feel ourselves moving through the stages quickly.

FEEDBACK FROM STAFF

The higher you are in the organization, the more difficult it is to get candid feedback about your own performance. Most performance appraisal processes don't allow for upward feedback. You must ask for it.

People learn at a very early age to not criticize parents, teachers, or bosses. This reluctance is hardwired into us. If you want people to go against their nature, you must ask for feedback again and again and again. The first time you ask for feedback, your staff may be skeptical. They may speculate that you just read *Feedback Toolkit*, and they may decide to lie low for a few days until you forget all about this nonsense.

If you receive any feedback at all, it may be only superficial. Take delight in what you get, and the next time you may get a little more. Giving feedback to one's supervisor is like deciding to swim in a strange pond. People want to test the waters. They put in a toe, and if that doesn't feel too bad, they put an entire foot in the water, and so on until they feel comfortable swimming freely. Allow people to dabble their toes in the water for a while.

Prepare

Consider why you need feedback from this person or group. Make sure there is a solid business reason in asking them to do something so potentially risky for their careers. Perhaps it will help you improve efficiency, conduct meetings, coordinate work among departments, or lead projects.

Consider this question: From your staff's point of view, what potential benefit might they see from giving you feedback.

Limit the request for feedback to one or two items. (You want to make this easy for them. If you ask for too much, you will overwhelm them and possibly yourself.)

Determine who you want to hear from. Perhaps you can get what you need from one person, from a series of one-to-one meetings, or from the entire group en masse. (If the thought of hearing feedback from a large group makes your stomach turn, trust that biological response, and limit feedback to one-on-one meetings.)

Present

Explain what you would like feedback on—and explain why the feedback is important to you.

If people are reluctant to speak, you might prime the pump by giving an example. "It seems to me that the way I jump from topic to topic in staff meetings might be confusing to you. Is that a problem? Would I do better to stick to a one-topic-at-a-time agenda?" This small example lets people know that you know there is a problem. That can make it easier for them to talk about this issue directly with you.

Listen

Listen to the responses. Ask questions to make sure you understand what they are saying. Don't defend yourself, make excuses, or blame someone else.

Engage in Dialogue

If the message you hear is heavy, don't engage in a dialogue. You need time to consider what you've just heard. If you speak now, you may make promises that you will regret later. Or worse, you may react defensively and lash out at the other person.

Plan for Action

Summarize what you have heard. If appropriate, tell them what you plan to do with the feedback.

Acknowledge

Thank them for their help.

Variation

Management of an office routinely meets with non-management staff to ask, "What are we doing that bugs you?" During these meetings, people often identify the hassles that inhibit effective work.

What to Watch For

One manager said, "I find it best to be specific on what I want feedback on by providing a recent example. Otherwise, the staff member is reluctant to dive in. Sticking to the specific incident seems to take the personal attack out of it, and makes it easier for me to listen." Another manager suggests, "Bosses need to model receiving feedback, even if they do it inelegantly."

FEEDBACK FROM YOUR BOSS

Not knowing where you stand with your boss can be a career killer. If you care about your career, you must manage this relationship as well.

Prepare

Consider this question: What is the potential benefit to your boss for giving you feedback? Make sure there is a solid business reason for engaging him or her in this discussion. Think about the one or two specific items you need feedback on in order to do your job brilliantly.

Present

State what you want clearly and specifically. Explain why this feedback is important to you.

Listen

Listen to his or her responses. Ask questions to make sure you understand what you are being told. Don't defend yourself.

Engage in Dialogue

If your boss delivers a heavy blow, don't engage in dialogue. You need time to consider what you've just heard. If you speak now, you may overpromise or react impulsively. Give yourself time to chew on the bad news and bring some calm back to your life.

But, let's say that the feedback makes sense to you and your boss invites more conversation about it. This is a good time to begin to explore that issue more deeply using skills of good dialogue.

Plan for Action

Summarize what you heard.

If you are ready, tell the boss what you plan to do based on what he or she just told you. If not, explain that you will think over what you heard and get back to him or her soon. Make sure you follow up on that commitment.

Acknowledge

Thank him or her for the help.

What to Watch For

Make sure there is a sound business reason. Most often you should have solid business reasons for having such a discussion with your boss. But let's say you are feeling insecure or uncertain about your position, and you would like to hear what your boss has to say. Unfortunately, that insecurity may make it difficult for you to engage in a highly personal exchange—a real catch-22.

Identifying a sound business reason for this feedback may make it easier to engage in a more difficult personal discussion at some later time. Or perhaps this business discussion may even begin to answer some of the unasked questions. For instance, your boss might say, "Well, Sylvia, I wouldn't worry about the Inco account. You probably won't be around long enough for it to matter much." And there you have your answer. Even though you may not like what you hear, at least now you can make decisions based on facts, not perceptions.

Watch out for your own level 3 reactions. Your ability to hear feedback from your boss will depend on the level 3 relationship. If you trust and respect your boss, you are more likely to be interested in what he or she has to say. You may even ask follow-up questions to make sure you really understand. In this instance, the feedback is important to you and so is the relationship.

On the other hand, if you don't trust or respect your boss, it may be extremely difficult to listen to him or her. An internal dialogue may take over. You might be saying to yourself, "Yeah, well who died and made you a god?" "Yeah, well consider the source. You're no saint yourself, bud."

Here's something you don't want to hear. Make yourself listen. Take notes. Paraphrase. Do anything you need to do to make sure you understand (level 1) what your boss is saying to you. Why? Because this person signs your paycheck. It's not fair. It may not be right, but it is reality. Get used to it.

FEEDBACK FROM PEERS

Increasingly, people find that they must rely heavily on peers or colleagues in other departments. Often, there is no reporting relationship in these peer exchanges, and therefore feedback is hard to get. It is in your best interests to keep these relationships open and clean. Your peers are your suppliers and your customers. Without good communication with suppliers, you may suffer delays and other problems. If internal customers are unhappy, you are not doing your job. Finally, peers talk. People are picked for plum assignments and considered for promotions based on informal grapevine assessments. You need to know what your peers are thinking and saying about you. They matter to your immediate success and to your career.

Prepare

Your peers fall into one of three camps:

Suppliers. These individuals or groups represent work units that supply you and your office with information, support, or resources.

Customers. These individuals or groups are major recipients of your products or services.

Project or task force. These people work with you on a team that examines some business issue.

Determine where each person or group fits. The questions you ask will be determined by your relationship.

Prepare specific questions for the meeting.

- Ask suppliers what they need from you to do their job most effectively. Even though you are the customer, you may be doing things that prevent your suppliers from giving you the best service.
- Ask customers what they like about your product or service, what they dislike, and what they would like to see changed.
- Ask project or task force members what you could be doing to serve the team more effectively. Consider using the term *ten-thousand-mile checkup* with this group (see "Project Debriefing" in Chapter 2).

Consider the best place to hold this meeting. Over coffee? At the end of a meeting? A conference call? Make it easy and relaxed. Keep it short.

Present

Explain what you would like feedback on and why it is important to you, as well as the potential benefit to them. Ask the questions you prepared.

Listen

Listen to their responses. Ask questions to make sure you understand what they are saying.

Engage in Dialogue

This may be an opportunity to engage in an informal expectations exchange with your peers. Since you led the way, others may now be willing to discuss ways in which you can assist each other in the future. Don't force this to happen. Pursue this course only if others seem interested.

Plan for Action

Summarize what you heard. If appropriate, tell them what you plan to do with the feedback.

Acknowledge

Thank them for their help.

Variation

The expectations exchange works well in peer relationships. Of course, you must get others to buy in before proceeding.

What to Watch For

Don't waste their time. Buy them a cup of coffee and ask a few questions. If some item looks like it could use an in-depth conversation, pull out your calendars and make a date.

Make it personal. Don't give them a lengthy survey. Most surveys are way too long and they cut out the personal connection. Peer-to-peer relationships work when level 3 trust and confidence is high. A face-to-face meeting gives you an opportunity to put money in that level 3 bank.

FEEDBACK FROM A COACH

Coaches can help you get focused—set goals and all that—and they can give you feedback that others may find hard to deliver. And the good news is that the coach is there for you. You don't have to worry that he or she will use what he or she learns against you.

The coach should be:

- Someone you trust and will listen to. Someone who has frequent opportunities to see you in action. Lots of studies indicate that we have deluded views of our own skills. For example, most of us think we are great drivers. Enough said. A coach needs to be able to see you in action.
- Someone who has nothing to gain or lose from engaging in these conversations.
- Definitely *not* someone who reports to you.

Prepare

Determine the areas in which you would like to receive coaching. Identify someone who meets the criteria listed above, and see if the person would be willing to work with you. Pick a regular time to meet and discuss your progress. For example, you might meet for lunch once a month.

Present

Remind him or her of what you are looking for.

During this meeting you might ask for feedback on a particular issue, or for help in meeting a future challenge. Or you might debrief an incident that didn't go as you had planned.

Listen

Listen to what your coach has to say. Listen deeply. Try to understand what he or she is telling you.

It is OK to defend yourself when meeting with your coach. However, once you have given the rationale as to why your actions were perfect, listen to what your coach has to say. Does he or she agree with your assessment?

Engage in Dialogue and Plan for Action

Together, brainstorm actions you might take in the future.

Acknowledge

Thank the person for the continued help.

Variation

Drive-by coaching. Although I work alone much of the time, I call on colleagues to coach me from afar. I explain the situation that has occurred, and once they stop laughing, I get their reactions and advice. I find it extremely helpful. So, even if the person who can be most helpful to you lives hundreds of miles away, you can still engage in productive exchanges over the phone. My buddy Max and I have been doing this for years. It's gotten to the point where one will call the other and ask, "Do you have ten minutes for some drive-by coaching? I'm about to go into an important meeting."

What to Watch For

Make sure your coach is willing to speak candidly to you. Coaches are people too, and they might have difficulty saying highly charged (level 2 or level 3) things to you.

FEEDBACK FROM QUESTIONNAIRES

You may have an opportunity to receive feedback through a formal questionnaire from your boss, peers, and staff. This information can be invaluable, but you must be ready to receive it.

Many training and development companies offer survey questionnaires that assess management performance on issues such as planning, motivation, and technical knowledge. They can be eye-opening and quite helpful. Often this process is referred to as 360° feedback in that you receive feedback from all around—boss, peers, and staff.

Selecting a Questionnaire

The following items may help you choose the appropriate questionnaire for your purposes. Examine the items on the questionnaire.

Measuring the right things. Will it measure the management practices on which you need feedback? If a questionnaire focuses primarily on performance in face-to-face meetings and you work with your staff over modems and phones, you may need to search for a better instrument.

Avoid vague categories. Be wary of questionnaires that simply use adjectives such as *forceful*, *directive*, and *supportive*. Adjectives are subject to too many varied interpretations. You may end up feeling bad without the benefit of learning what you could do differently. What possible good can it do to learn that 20% of your staff feel you are "adaptable" *and* that they don't like it? What does "adaptable" mean? What should you change? Look for items that delineate precisely what you are doing.

Determine how many people will fill it out. I have seen organizations offer managers well-written but poorly executed feedback tools that give managers a comparative score showing their own evaluation compared to what the boss has to say. Getting feedback from your boss can be helpful, but I like to cast the net more widely. What if that person happens to be a jerk? Look for a questionnaire that allows you to give it to multiple bosses, staff reporting to you, and peers.

Get help in interpreting the results. Survey feedback can be overwhelming. Make sure that the vendor or someone within your organization is skilled at interpreting the results of this particular tool. Don't go it alone; 360° feedback can be extremely powerful. You need to be assured that someone will walk you through the results.

Using the Questionnaire

Consider the following, once you decide to use a 360° questionnaire:

Choose people wisely. If you have the opportunity to choose who fills out the questionnaire, make sure you pick people who know you, people you respect, and people who will give you a candid assessment. The more care you take in selecting people, the higher the quality of feedback you will receive.

Some people choose others who they know will be hard on them. I don't know why they do that to themselves. Pick people who will give you a good picture of your leadership skills (or whatever skills you are measuring).

Determine what you want. Before you look at the results, identify what you want to learn. Are you interested in learning more about your leadership style? How well you keep people informed? How others view your project planning skills?

If you know the categories on the questionnaire, determine which areas are highest priority for your work before looking at the results.

Three-hundred-sixty-degree feedback can be overwhelming (remember SARA). If you go into the process knowing what you need, you are less likely to get lost in a mass of data or psychobabble.

Eat slowly and chew your food. Some 360° feedback instruments are long and cover many areas of management. Take your time with this feast. Read it. Walk away. Come back. Read some more. A few days later, look at the results again. Allow yourself time to take in the information. You can't eat the entire meal in a single sitting.

Look for similarities among groups. Notice patterns among the responses. Is everyone saying you are great at planning and need to work on your writing skills? Focus on these common themes.

Look for differences among groups. Be interested in why your boss rates you high in an area, while your staff rates you low.

Thank those who responded. Too often, feedback falls into a black hole. The respondents never know your reactions. At the very least, you owe them a thank you. Ideally, you will use the results to engage in further conversations.

Consider this a first step. Even the best questionnaires raise more questions. For example, the results may make you curious about why your peers see your project management skills so differently than you do.

Use other tools in this handbook to help you enrich this anonymous survey feedback. The tools for receiving feedback from a coach, from staff, and from peers may be especially helpful.

I want people to tell me the truth, even if it costs them their jobs.

—**Samuel Goldwyn**

Notes

1. Mark Frohman and Perry Pascarella, "American Management Operates in the Dark: *Industry Week* Magazine Survey," *Industry Week*, May 20, 1991, 25–29.
2. Employee Engagement: What's Your Engagement Ratio? Gallup.com (Washington, DC).
3. Daniel Goleman, *Emotional Intelligence* (New York, Bantam, 1995).
4. Chris Argyrus, *Overcoming Emotional Defenses* (Saddle River, NJ: Prentice Hall, 1990).
5. Rick Maurer, *Why Don't You Want What I Want?* (Austin, TX: Bard Press, 2002).
6. Tom Peters and Robert Waterman, *In Search of Excellence: Lessons from America's Best-Run Companies* (New York: Harper and Row, 1982).
7. John Case, *The Open Book Experience: Lessons From Over 100 Companies Who Successfully Transformed Themselves* (London: Nicholas Brealey Publishing, 1998).
8. Jack Stack, *The Great Game of Business* (New York: Currency/Doubleday, 1994).
9. John Scherer, "Job Related Adaptive Skills: Toward Personal Growth," in *Annual Handbook for Group Facilitators* (La Jolla, CA: University Associates, 1980).
10. Barry Goldwater, *Goldwater* (New York: Doubleday, 1988).

Index

E

E-mail, use of, 15–16
Embarrassment from feedback, 8
Emotional Intelligence, 2–3, 59
Emotional reaction to change, 2–3
Emotional support exercise, 29–31
Engagement, 24
Environment, impact on performance, 12
Evaluation meeting, 17–19
Exception, management by, 5–6
Excitement, 24
Expectations exchange, 19–22
Exploration, dialogue as, 12

F

Facilitating partnerships, 34
Fear, 2–3, 5–6, 24
Fear of change, 2–3
Feelings
    exploration of, 12
    stating, 8–9
Fight or flight reactions, 32
Focus on behavior, 8
Focus on customers, 3–4
Foundation building, 3–4
Frequency of feedback, 3–4
Frohman, Mark, 59
Functional skills, 43–44
Future, focusing on, 6

G

Getting to know staff, 28–29
Giving credit to others, 30
Giving feedback, 15–41
    acid bath feedback, 35–37
    advice, providing, 37–39
    annual reviews, 31–35
    debriefing, 22–25
    deep breathing during review, 33
    dehassling work environment, 17–19
    difficult feedback
        professional coaching, 35–37
        rehearsing, 35–37
    emotional support, 29–31
    expectations exchange, 19–22

fight or flight reactions, 32
getting to know staff, 28–29
identifying, analyzing, generalizing, 38–39
knowledge of staff, 28–29
Lean improvement process, 39–41
management by wandering around, 27–29
mentor, providing feedback as, 37–39
merit ratings, 31–35
military, use of after action reports, 24
mistakes, learning from, 15–17
open-book management, team feedback, 39–41
opportunities for learning, mistakes as, 15–17
performance reviews, 31–35
positive feedback for teams, 29–31
preparation of feedback, 37
professional coaching, rehearsing, 35–37
progress evaluation meeting, 17–19
progress evaluation of team, 25–27
project debriefing, 22–25
rehearsing, 35–37
relaxation during review, 33
Six Sigma improvement process, 39–41
virtual teams, 25–27
what are we doing meeting, 17–19
Goldwater, Barry, 44, 59
Goleman, Daniel, 2–3, 59
Grading, avoiding, 34
Gratitude, expression of, 46
The Great Game of Business, 39–40, 59
Ground rules, 13
    confidentiality, 13
    inflammatory comments, avoiding, 13
    respect, 13
Group brainstorming, 17
Guidelines to giving feedback, 6–9
    application, 9–11
    behavior, focus on, 8
    context, 7
    customer data, 6–7
    embarrassment from feedback, 8
    feelings, stating, 8–9
    future, focusing on, 6
    identification of business rationale, 6